A Fun Guide to Basketball

BY:

Deamer K Holdings

THIS BOOK BELONGS TO

PLAYFUL PLANET
KIDS SHOW

AI Disclaimer

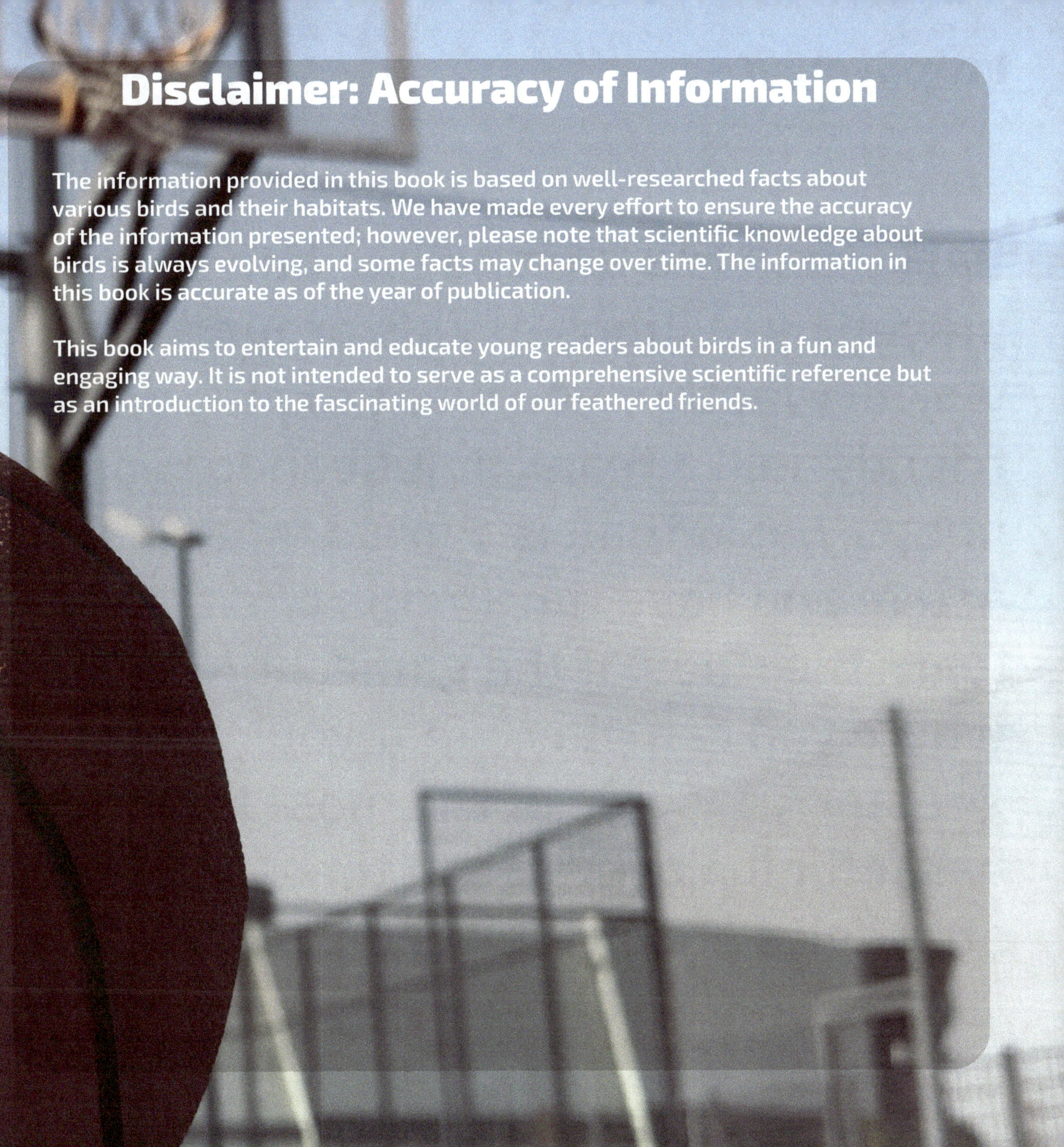

Disclaimer: Accuracy of Information

The information provided in this book is based on well-researched facts about various birds and their habitats. We have made every effort to ensure the accuracy of the information presented; however, please note that scientific knowledge about birds is always evolving, and some facts may change over time. The information in this book is accurate as of the year of publication.

This book aims to entertain and educate young readers about birds in a fun and engaging way. It is not intended to serve as a comprehensive scientific reference but as an introduction to the fascinating world of our feathered friends.

Introduction

Basketball is a fun and exciting sport played by millions of kids around the world! Whether you want to play with friends, join a team, or just shoot some hoops, basketball is a great way to stay active and have fun. In this book, you'll learn the rules of the game, how to play, where you can play, what you need to get started, some of the most famous basketball players of all time, and cool strategies and moves you can try!

Basketball is a fun and exciting sport played by millions of kids around the world! Whether you want to play with friends, join a team, or just shoot some hoops, basketball is a great way to stay active and have fun. In this book, you'll learn the rules of the game, how to play, where you can play, what you need to get started, some of the most famous basketball players of all time, and cool strategies and moves you can try!

Chapter 1:

The Basics of Basketball

Basketball is a team sport played between two teams of five players each. The goal is to score points by shooting the ball into the opposing team's basket while preventing them from scoring in yours. The team with the most points at the end of the game wins!

- Two hoops (one for each team)

- A three-point line (for long-range shots)

- A free-throw line (for penalty shots)

- A key (or paint area) (where players take close-range shots)

- A midcourt line (divides the court into two halves)

A basketball court has:

Chapter 2:

How to Play

Basketball is played in four quarters (or halves, depending on the level). Each team tries to move the ball down the court and score points. Here's how it works:

1. **Dribbling** – Bouncing the ball while moving.

2. **Passing** – Throwing the ball to a teammate.

3. **Shooting** – Aiming to score by getting the ball through the hoop.

4. **Defense** – Blocking, stealing, or stopping the opposing team from scoring.

5. **Rebounding** – Grabbing the ball after a missed shot.

Here's how it works:

Chapter 3:

The Rules of the Game

To play fair and have fun, here are some important rules to follow:

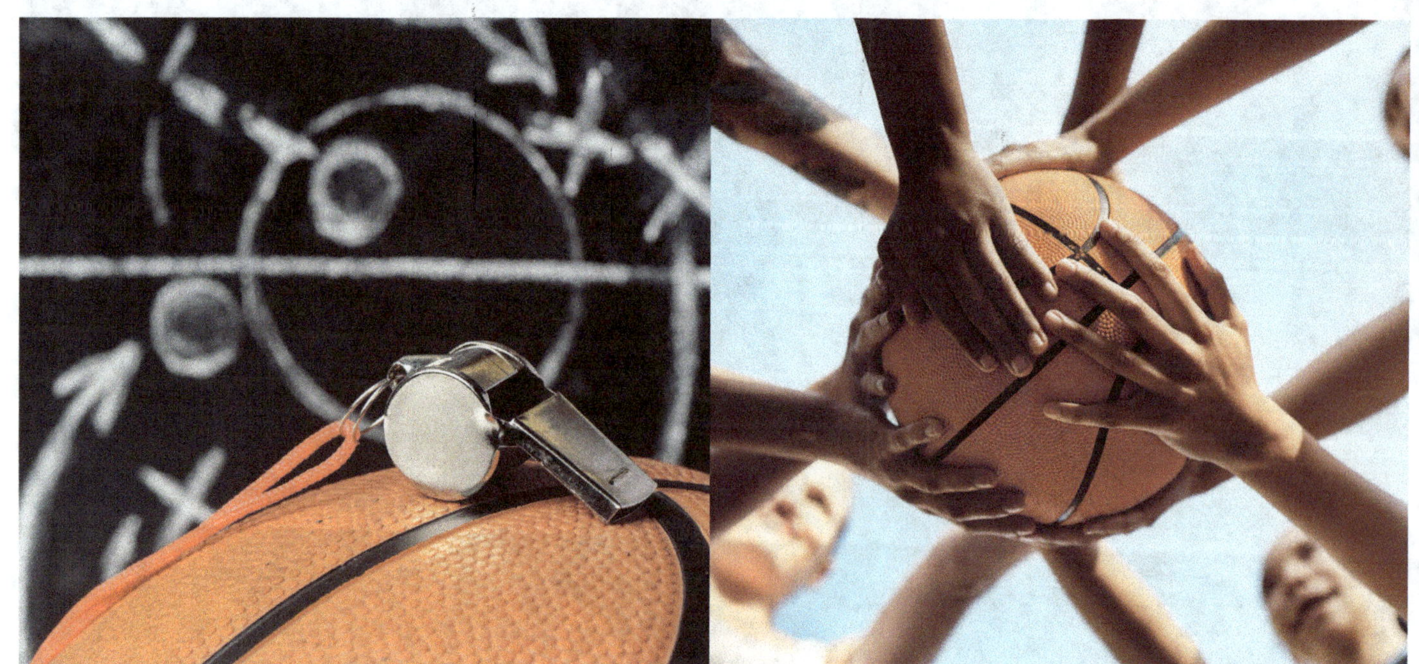

- The game starts with a jump ball.

- Players must dribble when moving with the ball.

- A shot inside the three-point line is worth two points.

- A shot outside the three-point line is worth three points.

- A free throw is worth one point.

- Each team has 24 seconds to take a shot (shot clock rule in professional play).

- Fouls happen when a player pushes, hits, or holds another player unfairly.

- Traveling occurs when a player moves without dribbling.

- Double dribble means stopping and starting dribbling again, which is not allowed.

important rules to follow:

Chapter 4:

Where to Play

You can play basketball almost anywhere! Here are some common places:

- Outdoor courts in parks or playgrounds.

- School gyms during PE class or after-school programs.

- Recreation centers that have leagues and teams.

- Driveways or backyards with a hoop attached to a garage.

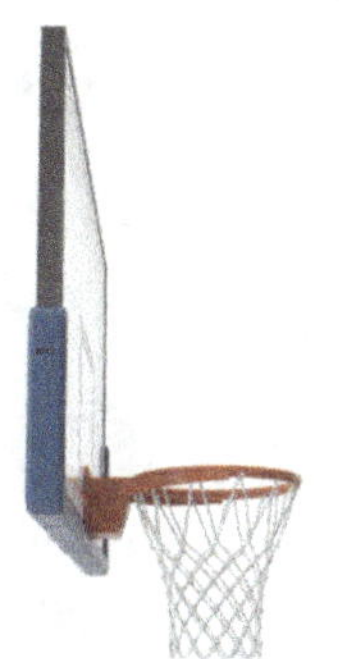

A basketball court:

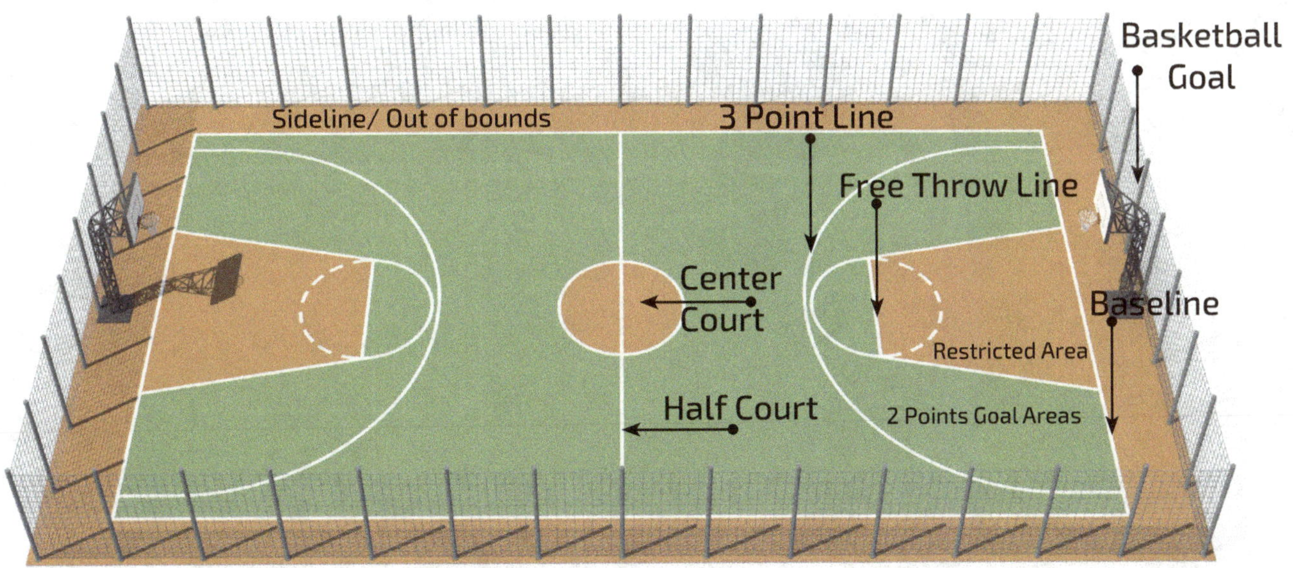

Chapter 5:

What You Need to Play
To start playing basketball, you only need a few things:

- A basketball (choose the right size for your age)

- A hoop and a court

- Comfortable clothes and sneakers with good grip

- Water bottle to stay hydrated

- A team or friends to play with

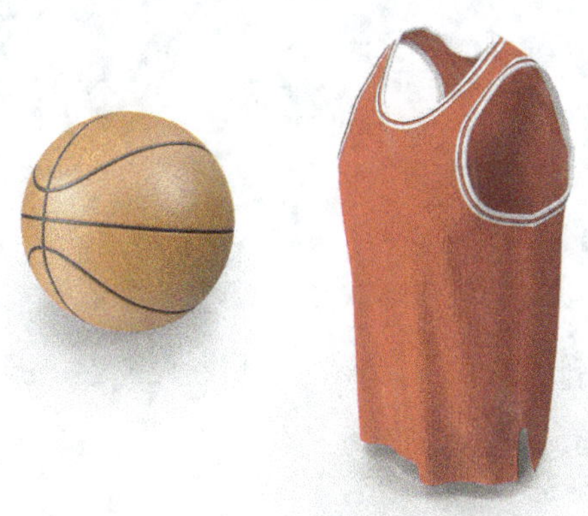

A basketball court has:

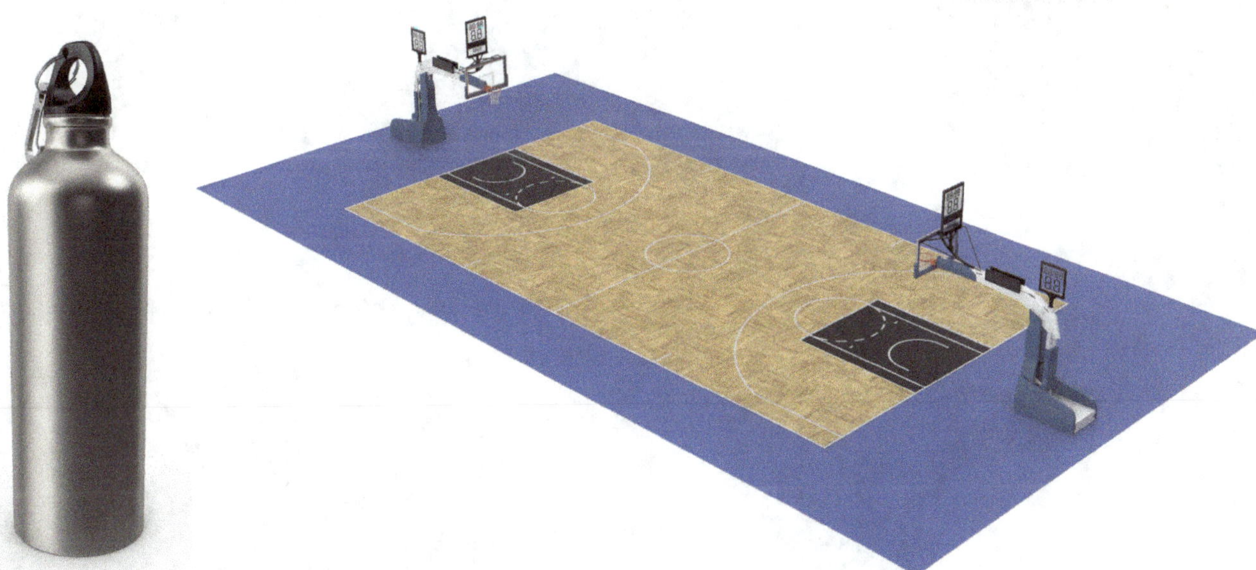

Chapter 6:

Basic Strategies and Cool Moves

To play better and impress your friends, here are some simple strategies and cool moves you can try:

- Pick and Roll – One player sets a screen (blocks a defender) to free up a teammate for an open shot or drive.

- Fast Break – Quickly moving the ball up the court before the defense can set up.

- Zone Defense – Instead of guarding one player, defenders cover specific areas of the court.

- Man-to-Man Defense – Each defender is assigned to cover a specific player on the opposing team.

Basic Strategies:

- **Crossover Dribble** – Quickly switching the ball from one hand to the other to get past a defender.

- **Behind-the-Back Dribble** – Dribbling the ball behind your back to avoid a defender.

- **Spin Move** – Spinning while dribbling to shake off a defender.

- **Step-Back Jumper** – Taking a quick step back before shooting to create space.

- **Euro Step** – A move where a player takes two quick steps in different directions to get past a defender for a layup.

Practice these moves, and you'll be a basketball pro in no time!

Cool Moves:

Chapter 7:

Famous Basketball Players

Many players have become legends of the game. Here are some of the most famous basketball stars:

- **Michael Jordan** – One of the greatest players ever, winning six NBA championships.

- **LeBron James** – A superstar known for his incredible skills and leadership.

- **Stephen Curry** – Famous for his amazing three-point shooting.

- **Kobe Bryant** – A legendary player known for his dedication and work ethic.

- **Lisa Leslie** – One of the best women's basketball players, a pioneer in the WNBA.

- **Magic Johnson** – Known for his fantastic passing and playmaking skills.

- **Shaquille O'Neal** – A dominant center who was nearly unstoppable.

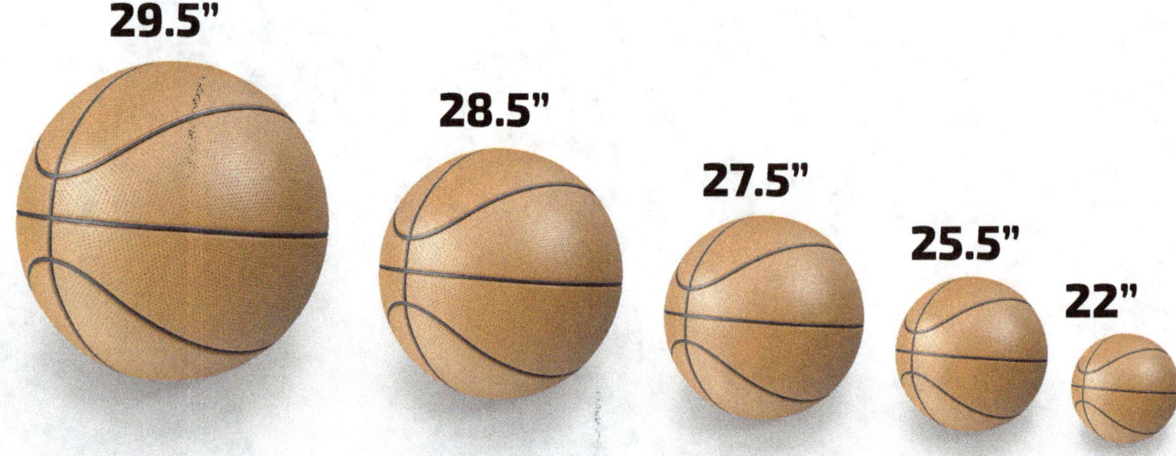

Size	Circumference	Weight	Recommended For
Size 7	29.5 inches (75 cm)	22 oz (620 g)	Men's professional, college, and high school basketball (NBA, NCAA, FIBA, NFHS)
Size 6	28.5 inches (72 cm)	20 oz (570 g)	Women's professional, college, and high school basketball (WNBA, NCAA, NFHS), and boys ages 12-14
Size 5	27.5 inches (70 cm)	17 oz (480 g)	Youth basketball, ages 9-11
Size 4	25.5 inches (65 cm)	14 oz (400 g)	Kids ages 5-8
Size 3	22 inches (56 cm)	10 oz (280 g)	Toddlers and beginners, ages 4 and under

Dimensions

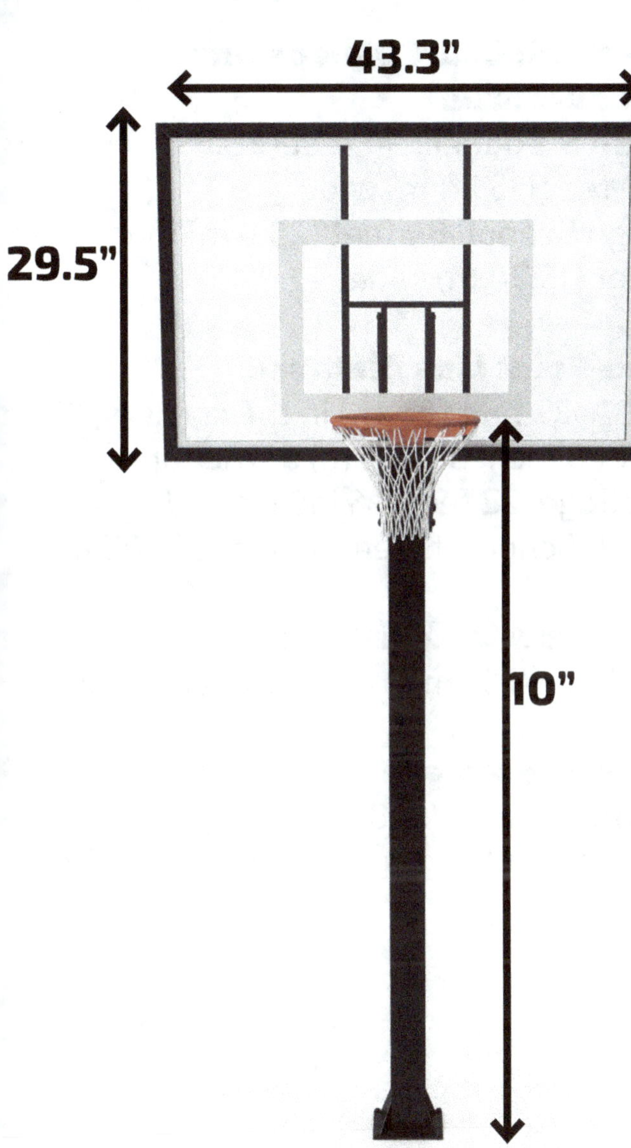

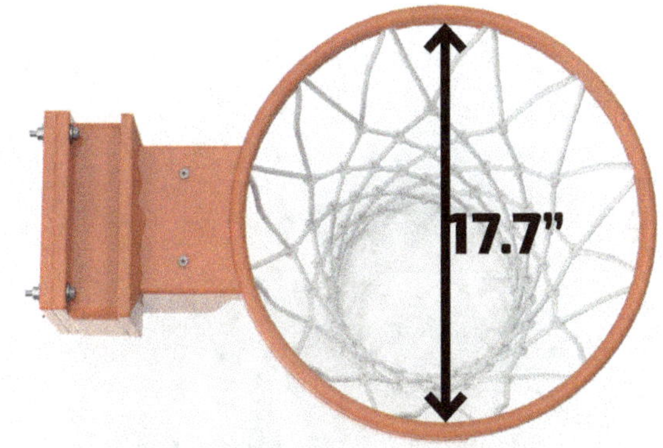

The standard basketball rim (hoop) size is:

- **Diameter:** 18 inches (45.72 cm)
- **Height from the ground:** 10 feet (3.05 meters)
- **Backboard width:** 72 inches (183 cm) (standard for professional courts)
- **Backboard height:** 42 inches (107 cm)

For youth basketball, hoop heights can be adjusted:

- 9 feet for younger players (ages 10-12)
- 8 feet for beginners (ages 7-9)

Basketball Court Dimensions

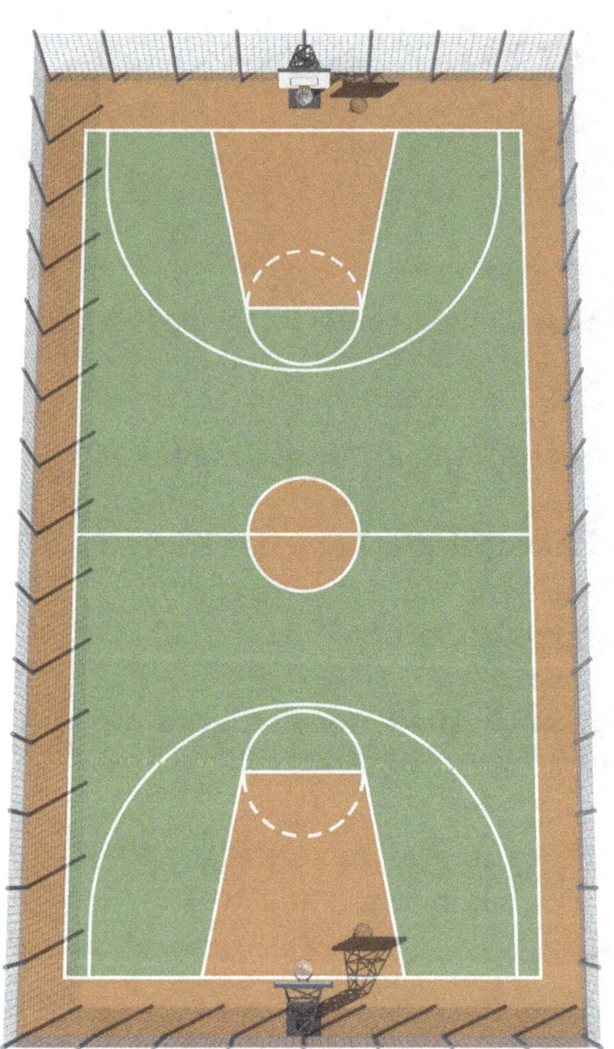

Basketball Court Dimensions
Full Court Size:
- NBA & College: 94 feet (28.65 m) long × 50 feet (15.24 m) wide
- High School: 84 feet (25.6 m) long × 50 feet (15.24 m) wide

Three-Point Line Distance:
- NBA: 22 feet (6.7 m) in the corners, 23 feet 9 inches (7.24 m) at the top
- College: 22 feet 1¾ inches (6.75 m)
- High School: 19 feet 9 inches (6.02 m)

Free Throw Line Distance:
- 15 feet (4.57 m) from the backboard

Key (Paint) Area Width:
- NBA: 16 feet (4.88 m)
- College & High School: 12 feet (3.66 m)

Basketball Court Dimensions

Basketball Hoop & Rim

- Rim Height: 10 feet (3.05 m) from the ground
- Rim Diameter: 18 inches (45.72 cm)
- Net Length: 15-18 inches (38-45 cm)

Backboard

- Width: 6 feet (1.83 m)
- Height: 3.5 feet (1.07 m)
- Inner Square on Backboard: 24 inches (width) × 18 inches (height)

Other Markings

- Baseline & Sideline: The boundaries of the court
- Center Circle: 12 feet (3.66 m) diameter, used for tip-off
- Restricted Area Arc (NBA & NCAA): 4 feet (1.22 m) from the basket (not in high school)
- No-Charge Zone: 4 feet (1.22 m) in the NBA, where defensive fouls don't apply

Basketball Stats Made Easy!

Did you know that basketball players have special numbers called stats that help track how well they play? Stats tell us how many points they score, how many rebounds they grab, and how many passes lead to a basket! Let's learn how stats work with some fun activities!

1. What Do These Stats Mean?
Draw a line to match the basketball stat with what it means:

Points (PTS) -"How many baskets a player makes"
Assists (AST)-"How many times a player passes the ball to help a teammate score"
Rebounds (REB)-"How many times a player grabs the ball after a missed shot"
Steals (STL) -"How many times a player takes the ball from the other team"
Blocks (BLK) - "How many times a player stops a shot from going in"

2. Keep Track of Your Own Stats!
Next time you play basketball, use this chart to track your stats!

Game #	Points (PTS)	Assists (AST)	Rebounds (REB)	Steals (STL)	Blocks (BLK)
1					
2					
3					
4					
5					

Basketball Stats Made Easy!

3. Who Had the Best Game?

Look at the stats of three players and decide who had the best game!

Player	Points (PTS)	Assists (AST)	Rebounds (REB)	Steals (STL)	Blocks (BLK)
Jake	12	3	7	2	1
Mia	8	4	5	1	0
Tony	5	2	6	3	2
Amber	15	5	4	2	8
Nailah	30	6	8	3	5

Questions:

1. Which player scored the most points?

2. Who had the most assists?

3. Which player had the best defense (steals + blocks)?

4. If a rebound is worth 1 point and an assist is worth 2 points, whose total

5. contribution is the highest?

Basketball Scavenger Hunt

Next time you're at a game or watching one on TV, see if you can spot these things happening:

☐ **A player dribbling the ball**
☐ **A referee blowing the whistle**
☐ **A three-point shot**
☐ **A slam dunk**
☐ **A team huddle**
☐ **A player making a free throw**

Basketball Court Dimensions

Test your basketball knowledge with these fun questions!

1. How many players are on a basketball team during a game?
    a) 4
    b) 5
    c) 6
2. What is it called when a player bounces the ball while moving?
    a) Passing
    b) Dribbling
    c) Shooting
3. How many points is a three-pointer worth?
    a) 1
    b) 2
    c) 3
4. Who is famous for wearing the number 23 and winning six championships?
    a) Stephen Curry
    b) LeBron James
    c) Michael Jordan

Conclusion

Basketball is a fantastic sport that anyone can play and enjoy! Whether you're playing for fun, joining a team, or dreaming of becoming a pro, basketball helps you stay active, make friends, and learn teamwork. Now that you know the rules, strategies, and cool moves, grab a ball and start playing!

- **Dribble** – Bouncing the ball while moving.

- **Layup** – A close-range shot taken while running toward the basket.

- **Rebound** – Catching the ball after a missed shot.

- **Assist** – A pass that leads directly to a basket.

- **Defense** – The team without the ball trying to stop the other team from scoring.

Happy playing!

Glossary

Design your own jersey

Design your own jersey

Design your own jersey

Design your own jersey

AMAZON STORE
YOUTUBE SUBSCRIBE
PLAYFUL PLANET KIDS SHOW
ROCK-IT

AMAZON STORE
YOUTUBE SUBSCRIBE
PLAYFUL PLANET KIDS SHOW
PIPPY

AMAZON STORE
YOUTUBE SUBSCRIBE
PLAYFUL PLANET KIDS SHOW
STARSHINE

PLAYFUL PLANET KIDS SHOW
YOUTUBE
AMAZON STORE
SUBSCRIBE
ASTROID

AMAZON STORE
YOUTUBE
SUBSCRIBE
PLAYFUL PLANET KIDS SHOW
SUNNY

PLAYFUL
PLANET
KIDS SHOW
AMAZON
STORE
YOUTUBE
SUBSCRIBE
LUNAR

PLAYFUL PLANET
KIDS SHOW
AMAZON STORE
YOUTUBE SUBSCRIBE

CERTIFICATE OF COMPLETION.

THIS CERTIFICATE IS PRESENTED

GREAT JOB!

DATE

Parents and caregivers are invited to watch alongside their little ones. We encourage you to actively participate, imitate sounds, and engage in the activities shown on the screen to enhance your child's learning and development.

Welcome to **[Preschool with Pippy]**, where the magic of reading and writing begins!
At **age 3**, your child is embarking on an exciting journey of literacy development. By now, they should be showing signs of readiness for reading and writing, including:

- **Language Skills:** Your child may be using more complex sentences and expanding their vocabulary daily. They may also enjoy rhymes, songs, and storytelling.

- **Print Awareness:** Look for signs that your child recognizes letters and numbers in their environment, such as on signs, labels, and books. They may also be interested in scribbling and drawing, demonstrating an early understanding of writing.

- **Interest in Books:** Encourage your child's love for books by reading together regularly. They may enjoy simple stories with colorful illustrations and may even begin to "read" familiar books by memory.

- **Fine Motor Skills:** Developing fine motor skills is crucial for writing readiness. Activities such as drawing, coloring, and tracing lines can help strengthen these skills.

- **Curiosity and Engagement:** Your child's curiosity about the world around them is blossoming. Encourage their natural curiosity by providing opportunities for exploration and hands-on learning experiences.

As you read and explore The preschool with Pippy Series together, remember to celebrate your child's progress and enjoy this special time of growth and discovery.

Happy reading!

Playful Planet Kids Show.